juices,
smoothies
and
shakes

Your Promise of Success

Welcome to the world of Confident Cooking, created for you in our
test kitchen, where recipes are double-tested by our team
of home economists to achieve a high standard of success.

PERIPLUS

MELON FREEZIE

Preparation time: 20 minutes
  + freezing time
Makes 4 x 300 ml glasses

500 g rockmelon
500 g honeydew melon
1 cup ice (12 ice cubes)
2 cups (500 ml) orange juice

1 Remove the rind and seeds from the melons. Cut the flesh into pieces and mix in a blender for 1 minute, or until smooth.
2 Add the ice and orange juice and blend for a further 30 seconds. Transfer to a large shallow plastic dish and freeze for 3 hours.
3 Return the mixture to the blender and blend quickly until smooth. Serve immediately with straws and long spoons.

NUTRITION: Protein 1.75 g; Fat 0.88 g; Carbohydrate 30 g; Dietary Fibre 2.63 g; Cholesterol 0 g; 540 kJ (130 cal)

Hint: Roughly break up the ice cubes first by placing them in a clean tea towel and hitting on a hard surface.

LEMON, LIME AND SODA WITH CITRUS ICE CUBES

Preparation time: 15 minutes
  + freezing time
Makes 2 x 375 ml glasses, 8 ice cubes

1 lemon
1 lime
2¹/₂ tablespoons lemon juice
²/₃ cup (170 ml) lime juice cordial
2¹/₂ cups (625 ml) soda water, chilled

1 Using a sharp knife, remove the peel and white pith from the lemon and lime. On a chopping board, cut between the membranes to release the segments. Place a lemon and lime segment in each hole of an ice cube tray and cover with water. Freeze for 2–3 hours or overnight until firm.
2 Combine the lemon juice, lime juice cordial and soda water.
3 Pour into long, chilled glasses with the ice cubes.

NUTRITION: Protein 0.5 g; Fat 0 g;
Carbohydrate 40 g; Dietary Fibre 1.5 g;
Cholesterol 0 g; 715 kJ (170 cal)

CARROT COCKTAIL
Preparation time: 10 minutes
Makes 2 x 375 ml glasses

10–12 carrots, quartered lengthways
1/2 cup (125 ml) pineapple juice
1/2 cup (125 ml) orange juice
1–2 teaspoons honey, to taste
8 ice cubes

1 Using the plunger, push the carrot pieces through a juicer.
2 Combine the carrot juice with the remaining ingredients in a jug and serve.

NUTRITION: Protein 4 g; Fat 0.5 g; Carbohydrate 40 g; Dietary Fibre 15 g; Cholesterol 0 g; 770 kJ (185 cal)

FRESH PINEAPPLE JUICE WITH MANDARIN SORBET
Preparation time: 10 minutes
+ chilling time
Makes 2 x 375 ml glasses

1 (2.4 kg) pineapple, peeled and cored
1 cup (250 ml) ginger ale
4 scoops mandarin sorbet

1 Roughly chop the pineapple flesh then push through a juicer.
2 Combine the pineapple juice and the ginger ale in a large jug. Chill.
3 Pour the juice into chilled glasses and top with scoops of sorbet.

NUTRITION: Protein 13 g; Fat 2.5 g; Carbohydrate 115 g; Dietary Fibre 25 g; Cholesterol 5 g; 2251 kJ (540 cal)

GINGER, LEMON AND MINT SOOTHER
Preparation time: 10 minutes
+ infusing + chilling time
Makes 4 x 250 ml glasses

2 cm (15 g) piece fresh ginger, finely sliced
1/2 cup (125 ml) lemon juice
2 1/2 tablespoons honey
1 tablespoon fresh mint leaves

1 Place the ginger, lemon juice, honey and mint into a heatproof jug and cover with 3 cups (750 ml) boiling water. Leave to infuse for 2–3 hours, or until cold.
2 When the mixture is cold, strain into another jug and chill in the refrigerator.
3 Serve in tall, chilled glasses over ice.

NUTRITION: Protein 0.21g; Fat 0 g; Carbohydrate 15 g; Dietary Fibre 0 g; Cholesterol 0 g; 260 kJ (62 cal)

Note: This drink is delicious served the next day as all the flavours will have time to infuse together.

Ginger, Lemon and Mint Soother (top), Carrot Cocktail (left), Fresh Pineapple Juice with Mandarin Sorbet (right).

PASSIONFRUIT AND VANILLA ICE CREAM WHIP

Preparation time: 10 minutes
Makes 2 x 375 ml glasses

4 passionfruit
100 g passionfruit yoghurt
2 cups (500 ml) milk
1 tablespoon caster sugar
2 scoops vanilla ice cream

1 Scoop out the pulp from the passionfruit and push through a sieve to remove the seeds. Place into the blender with the yoghurt, milk, sugar and ice cream and blend until smooth.

2 Pour into tall glasses and serve with an extra scoop of ice cream, if desired.

NUTRITION: Protein 13 g; Fat 14 g; Carbohydrate 35 g; Dietary Fibre 5.5 g; Cholesterol 45 g; 1335 kJ (318 cal)

CRANBERRY AND VANILLA ICE CREAM SPIDER

Preparation time: 15 minutes
Makes 4 x 250 ml glasses

2 cups (500 ml) cranberry juice
2 cups (500 ml) soda water
4 scoops vanilla ice cream
3/4 cup (185 ml) cream
1 tablespoon caster sugar
20 g flaked almonds, toasted

1 Combine the juice and soda water in a jug. Add a scoop of ice cream to each tall glass. Pour the juice and soda over the ice cream.

2 Whip the cream and sugar until soft peaks form. Spoon over the juice and soda and top with a sprinkle of almonds.

NUTRITION: Protein 2.5 g; Fat 25 g; Carbohydrate 15 g; Dietary Fibre 3 g; Cholesterol 6.7 g; 540 kJ (130 cal)

MELON SHAKE

Preparation time: 15 minutes
Makes 2 x 375 ml glasses

500 g rockmelon, peeled and seeded
2 tablespoons honey
1 1/2 cups (375 ml) milk
5 scoops vanilla ice cream
ground nutmeg, to garnish

1 Cut the rockmelon into 2 cm
pieces and place in a blender. Mix
for 30 seconds, or until smooth.
2 Add the honey, milk and ice
cream and blend for a further
10–20 seconds, or until well
combined and smooth.
3 Serve sprinkled with nutmeg.

NUTRITION: Protein 10 g; Fat 15 g;
Carbohydrate 55 g; Dietary Fibre 2.5 g;
Cholesterol 42 g; 1590 kJ (380 cal)

WATERMELON SMOOTHIE

Preparation time: 15 minutes
Makes 4 x 250 ml glasses

600 g watermelon, skinned and seeded
1 cup (250 ml) milk
1/2 cup (125 g) yoghurt
1 tablespoon caster sugar
2 scoops vanilla ice cream

1 Blend the watermelon, milk,
yoghurt and caster sugar in a
blender until smooth.
2 Add the ice cream and blend
for a further few seconds, or
until the mixture is frothy.
Serve immediately.

NUTRITION: Protein 4.5 g; Fat 5 g;
Carbohydrate 20 g; Dietary Fibre 1 g;
Cholesterol 17 g; 590 kJ (140 cal)

PEACHY EGG NOG

Preparation time: 10 minutes
 + cooling + chilling time
Total cooking time: 8 minutes
Makes 4 x 225 ml glasses

2 eggs, separated
1/4 cup (60 ml) milk
1/4 cup (60 g) caster sugar
1/3 cup (80 ml) cream
13/4 cups (440 ml) peach nectar
2 tablespoons orange juice
ground nutmeg, to garnish

1 Beat the egg yolks, milk and half
the sugar in a bowl and place over
a pan of simmering water—do not
allow the base of the bowl to
touch the water. Cook, stirring,
for 8 minutes, or until the custard
thickens. Remove from the heat
and cover the surface with plastic
wrap. Cool.
2 Beat the egg whites until frothy.
Add the remaining sugar, to taste,
then beat until stiff peaks form. In
a separate bowl, whip the cream
until soft peaks form.
3 Gently fold the egg whites and
cream into the cooled custard. Stir
in the nectar and juice. Cover and
chill for 2 hours.
4 Beat the mixture lightly, pour
into glasses and sprinkle with
nutmeg.

NUTRITION: Protein 5 g; Fat 12 g;
Carbohydrate 25 g; Dietary Fibre 1.5 g;
Cholesterol 120 g; 940 kJ (225 cal)

SUMMER BUTTERMILK SMOOTHIE

Preparation time: 10 minutes
Makes 2 x 375 ml glasses

350 g rockmelon
2 peaches, peeled and sliced
150 g strawberries, roughly chopped
4 mint leaves
1/2 cup (125 ml) buttermilk
1/2 cup (125 ml) orange juice
1–2 tablespoons honey

1 Remove the rind and seeds from the melon and cut the flesh into pieces.
2 Place the rockmelon, peaches, strawberries and mint leaves in a blender and blend until smooth.
3 Add the buttermilk, orange juice and 1 tablespoon of the honey and blend to combine. Taste for sweetness and add more honey if needed.

NUTRITION: Protein 6 g; Fat 2 g; Carbohydrate 50 g; Dietary Fibre 5 g; Cholesterol 6 g; 978 kJ (235 cal)

Note: This drink should be consumed within 3 hours of being made in order to retain colour and freshness of flavour.

PASSIONFRUIT LIME CRUSH
Preparation time: 10 minutes
Makes 4 x 250 ml glasses

1/2 cup (125 g) passionfruit pulp
3/4 cup (185 ml) lime juice cordial
3 cups (750 ml) ginger ale
crushed ice

1 Combine the pulp, cordial and ginger ale in a jug. Mix well.
2 Pour into glasses filled with crushed ice. Serve immediately.

NUTRITION: Protein 0.5 g; Fat 0 g;
Carbohydrate 40 g; Dietary Fibre 1.7 g;
Cholesterol 0 g; 700 kJ (170 cal)

PEACHY KEEN
Preparation time: 15 minutes
Makes 2 x 350 ml glasses

3/4 cup (185 g) low-fat peach and mango yoghurt
3/4 cup (185 ml) apricot nectar, chilled
1/2 cup (60 g) fresh or frozen raspberries
1 1/2 cups (300 g) diced fresh peaches
8 large ice cubes
fresh peach wedges, to serve

1 Place the yoghurt, nectar, fruit and ice in a blender and blend until smooth.
2 Serve with the peach wedges.

NUTRITION: Protein 7 g; Fat 0.5 g;
Carbohydrate 35 g; Dietary Fibre 3.5 g;
Cholesterol 3 g; 770 kJ (185 cal)

BANANA SOY LATTE
Preparation time: 10 minutes
Makes 4 x 250 ml glasses

1 3/4 cups (440 ml) coffee-flavoured soy milk, chilled
2 bananas, sliced
8 large ice cubes
1 teaspoon drinking chocolate
1/4 teaspoon ground cinnamon

1 Place the soy milk and sliced bananas in a blender and process until smooth.
2 With the blender running, add the ice cubes one at a time until well incorporated and the desired consistency is reached.
3 Pour into tall chilled glasses and sprinkle generously with the drinking chocolate and ground cinnamon.

NUTRITION: Protein 45 g; Fat 4 g;
Carbohydrate 18 g; Dietary Fibre 2 g;
Cholesterol 0 g; 520 kJ (125 cal)

Passionfruit Lime Crush (top), Peachy Keen (left), Banana Soy Latte (right).

BLACKCURRANT CRUSH
Preparation time: 10 minutes
Makes 4 x 300 ml glasses

3 cups (750 ml) apple and
  blackcurrant juice
2 cups (500 ml) soda water
1 tablespoon caster sugar
150 g blueberries
ice cubes, to serve

1 Place the apple and blackcurrant
juice, soda water, sugar and
blueberries into a blender and blend
until smooth.
2 Serve in chilled glasses over ice.

NUTRITION: Protein 0.5 g; Fat 0.5 g;
Carbohydrate 30 g; Dietary Fibre 0.5 g;
Cholesterol 0 g; 515 kJ (125 cal)

Note: If you have a really good blender,
you may wish to add the ice cubes when
blending the other ingredients to make
a slushy.

APRICOT WHIP
Preparation time: 20 minutes
Makes 3 x 250 ml glasses

75 g dried apricots
1/2 cup (125 g) apricot yoghurt
2/3 cup (170 ml) light coconut milk
1 1/4 cups (315 ml) milk
1 tablespoon honey
1 scoop vanilla ice cream
flaked coconut, toasted, to garnish

1 Cover the apricots with boiling
water and soak for 15 minutes.
Drain and roughly chop. Place the
apricots, yoghurt, coconut milk,
milk, honey and ice cream in a
blender and blend until smooth.
2 Pour into tall, chilled glasses and
sprinkle with the flaked coconut.

NUTRITION: Protein 7.5 g; Fat 12 g;
Carbohydrate 25 g; Dietary Fibre 3 g;
Cholesterol 20 g; 950 kJ (225 cal)

MANGO SMOOTHIE WITH FRESH BERRIES

Preparation time: 10 minutes
Makes 4 x 250 ml glasses

2 (800 g) fresh mangoes, peeled
    and seeded
1/2 cup (125 ml) milk
1 cup (250 ml) buttermilk
1 tablespoon caster sugar
2 scoops mango gelati or sorbet
50 g blueberries

1 Place the mango, milk, buttermilk, sugar and gelati in a blender and blend until smooth.
2 Pour into chilled glasses and serve garnished with the blueberries.

NUTRITION: Protein 6 g; Fat 3.5 g; Carbohydrate 40 g; Dietary Fibre 3 g; Cholesterol 11 g; 858 kJ (205 cal)

BANANA DATE SMOOTHIE

Preparation time: 10 minutes
Makes 2 x 350 ml glasses

1 cup (250 g) low-fat plain yoghurt
1/2 cup (125 ml) skim milk
1/2 cup (50 g) fresh dates, pitted
    and chopped
2 bananas, sliced
8 ice cubes

1 Place the yoghurt, milk, dates, banana and ice cubes in a blender. Blend until the mixture is smooth and the ice cubes have been well incorporated.
2 Serve in chilled glasses.

NUTRITION: Protein 10 g; Fat 0.5 g; Carbohydrate 48 g; Dietary Fibre 5 g; Cholesterol 7 g; 1013 kJ (240 cal)

CORDIALS

These modern fruit-flavoured cordials should keep well for several months in the fridge.

BITTER LEMON

Place 2 cups (500 ml) lemon juice and 1 cup (250 g) caster sugar in a pan. Stir over medium heat until the sugar has dissolved. Increase the heat and simmer rapidly, without stirring, for 6 minutes, or until the liquid reaches 85°C (185°F). Stir through ½ teaspoon bitters. Pour into a new bottle and lay on its side to sterilise the lid. Refrigerate. *Makes 2 cups (500 ml).*

APPLE AND BLACKBERRY

Place 2 cups (500 ml) fresh apple juice, 300 g frozen blackberries and 1 cup (250 g) caster sugar in a pan. Stir over medium heat until the sugar has dissolved. Increase the heat and simmer rapidly, without stirring, for 12 minutes, or until the liquid reaches 85°C (185°F). Strain out the seeds. Pour into a new bottle and lay on its side to sterilise the lid. Refrigerate. *Makes 3 cups (750 ml).*

PASSIONFRUIT AND COCONUT

Place 1 cup (250 g) passionfruit pulp, 1 cup (250 ml) water, $^3/_4$ cup (185 g) caster sugar and $^1/_4$ teaspoon coconut essence in a pan. Stir over medium heat until the sugar has dissolved. Simmer rapidly, without stirring, for 6 minutes, or until the liquid reaches 85°C (185°F). Pour into a new bottle and lay on its side to sterilise the lid. Refrigerate. *Makes* $1^3/_4$ *cups (440 ml).*

RASPBERRY

Place 300 g fresh or frozen raspberries, $^3/_4$ cup (185 ml) water and $^3/_4$ cup (185 g) caster sugar in a pan. Stir over medium heat until the sugar has dissolved. Increase the heat and simmer rapidly, without stirring, for 6 minutes, or until the liquid reaches 85°C (185°F). Strain and discard the seeds, then stir through 100 g fresh or frozen raspberries. Pour into a new bottle and lay on its side to sterilise the lid. Refrigerate. *Makes* $1^1/_2$ *cups (375 ml).*

15

ORANGE AND CARDAMOM HERBAL TEA

Preparation time: 10 minutes
  + infusing + chilling time
Total cooking time: 10 minutes
Makes 2 x 275 ml glasses

3 cardamom pods
1 cup (250 ml) fresh orange juice
3 strips orange rind
2 tablespoons caster sugar

1 Place the cardamom pods on a chopping board and press with the side of a large knife to crack them open. Place the cardamom, orange juice, rind, sugar and 2 cups (500 ml) water in a pan and stir over medium heat for 10 minutes, or until the sugar has dissolved. Bring to the boil then remove from the heat.
2 Leave to infuse for 2–3 hours, or until cold. Chill in the refrigerator. Strain and serve over ice.

NUTRITION: Protein 0.3 g; Fat 0.5 g; Carbohydrate 35 g; Dietary Fibre 0.25 g; Cholesterol 0 g; 590 kJ (140 cal)

VIRGIN MARY

Preparation time: 5 minutes
Makes 4 x 200 ml glasses

3 cups (750 ml) tomato juice
1 tablespoon Worcestershire sauce
2 tablespoons lemon juice
$^{1}/_{4}$ teaspoon ground nutmeg
few drops Tabasco sauce
1 cup ice (12 ice cubes)
2 lemon slices, halved

1 Place the tomato juice,
Worcestershire sauce, lemon juice,
nutmeg and Tabasco sauce in a
large jug and stir until combined.
2 Place the ice cubes in a blender
and blend for 30 seconds, or until
the ice is crushed down to $^{1}/_{2}$ cup.
3 Pour the tomato juice mixture
into serving glasses and add the
crushed ice and lemon slices.
Season with salt and pepper
before serving.

NUTRITION: Protein 1.5 g; Fat 0 g;
Carbohydrate 8 g; Dietary Fibre 0.5 g;
Cholesterol 0 g; 175 kJ (40 cal)

RUBY GRAPEFRUIT AND LEMON SORBET FIZZ

Preparation time: 5 minutes
Makes 4 x 250 ml glasses

2 cups (500 ml) ruby grapefruit juice
I cup (250 ml) soda water
I tablespoon caster sugar
4 scoops lemon sorbet

1 Combine the juice, soda water and sugar in a jug. Refrigerate.
2 Pour into chilled glasses and top with a scoop of lemon sorbet.

NUTRITION: Protein 1.14 g; Fat 0.84 g; Carbohydrate 15 g; Dietary Fibre 0 g; Cholesterol 2.5 g; 305 kJ (75 cal)

BLUE MAPLE

Preparation time: 10 minutes
Makes 2 x 375 ml glasses

I cup (200 g) low-fat blueberry
   fromage fraîs
3/4 cup (185 ml) low-fat milk
I tablespoon maple syrup
1/2 teaspoon ground cinnamon
300 g frozen blueberries

1 Combine the fromage fraîs, milk, maple syrup, cinnamon and 250 g blueberries in a blender until smooth.
2 Pour into chilled glasses and top with the remaining blueberries.

NUTRITION: Protein 11 g; Fat 0.5 g; Carbohydrate 0 g; Dietary Fibre 2.7 g; Cholesterol 7 g; 942 kJ (225 cal)

APPLE AND CINNAMON HERBAL TEA INFUSION

Preparation time: 10 minutes
   + cooling + chilling time
Total cooking time: 15 minutes
Makes 2 x 300 ml glasses

4 (600 g) golden delicious apples,
   roughly chopped
I cinnamon stick
3–4 tablespoons soft brown sugar
ice cubes, to serve

1 Place the apple, cinnamon stick, brown sugar and 1 litre water in a pan. Bring to the boil, then reduce the heat and simmer for 10–15 minutes, or until the flavours have infused and the apples have softened.
2 Remove from the heat, cool slightly, then chill in the refrigerator until cold.
3 When cold, strain and serve over lots of ice.

NUTRITION: Protein 1 g; Fat 0.3 g; Carbohydrate 70 g; Dietary Fibre 5.5 g; Cholesterol 0 g; 1165 kJ (280 cal)

Apple and Cinnamon Herbal Tea Infusion (top), **Ruby Grapefruit and Lemon Sorbet Fizz** (left), **Blue Maple** (right).

MANDARIN AND MANGO CHILL

Preparation time: 15 minutes
+ freezing time
Makes 2 x 375 ml glasses

1 mango, cut into slices
2 cups (500 ml) mandarin juice
1/2 cup (125 ml) lime juice cordial
1 1/2 cups (375 ml) soda water
2 tablespoons caster sugar
ice cubes, to serve

1 Freeze the mango for about
1 hour, or until semi-frozen.
2 Combine the juice, cordial, soda
water and sugar in a jug.
3 Place the mango slices and some
ice cubes into each glass, then pour
in the juice mix.

NUTRITION: Protein 3 g; Fat 0.5 g;
Carbohydrate 110 g; Dietary Fibre 4.5 g;
Cholesterol 0 g; 1885 kJ (450 cal)

WILD BERRIES

Preparation time: 10 minutes
Makes 4 x 200 ml glasses

1 cup (250 g) low-fat strawberry
yoghurt
1/2 cup (125 ml) cranberry juice, chilled
250 g strawberries, hulled and
quartered
125 g frozen raspberries

1 Combine the yoghurt and
cranberry juice in a blender. Add
the strawberries and 80 g of the
raspberries. Blend until smooth.
2 Pour into chilled glasses and
top with the remaining frozen
raspberries. Serve with a spoon as
it is quite thick.

NUTRITION: Protein 4 g; Fat 0.5 g;
Carbohydrate 10 g; Dietary Fibre 3.5 g;
Cholesterol 1.5 g; 295 kJ (70 cal)

PLUM AND PRUNE TANG

Preparation time: 10 minutes
Makes 4 x 200 ml glasses

1 cup (250 g) low-fat vanilla yoghurt
1/2 cup (125 ml) buttermilk
1 1/4 cups (315 ml) milk
1 cup (150 g) prunes, pitted and diced
1/2 cup (200 g) diced fresh plums
8 large ice cubes

1 Place the yoghurt, buttermilk, milk, prunes, plums and ice cubes in a blender. Blend until the mixture is smooth and the ice cubes have been well incorporated.
2 Serve immediately.

NUTRITION: Protein 7 g; Fat 2.74 g; Carbohydrate 30 g; Dietary Fibre 4 g; Cholesterol 12 g; 740 kJ (175 cal)

BIG BOLD BANANA

Preparation time: 15 minutes
Makes 4 x 375 ml glasses

3 cups (750 ml) soy milk, chilled
125 g soft silken tofu
4 very ripe bananas, sliced
1 tablespoon honey
1 tablespoon vanilla essence
1 tablespoon carob powder (see Note)

1 Combine the soy milk and tofu in a blender. Add the banana, honey, vanilla essence and carob powder. Blend until smooth.
2 Serve in tall chilled glasses with a long spoon.

NUTRITION: Protein 8.5 g; Fat 7 g; Carbohydrate 42 g; Dietary Fibre 3.75 g; Cholesterol 0 g; 1060 kJ (253 cal)

Note: Carob powder is available from health food stores.

ORANGE AND GINGER TEA COOLER

Preparation time: 10 minutes
+ infusing + chilling time
Makes 2 x 375 ml glasses

1 small orange
1/2–1 tablespoon Darjeeling tea leaves
1 cup (250 ml) ginger beer
8 thin slices glacé ginger
2 tablespoons sugar
4–6 ice cubes
mint leaves, to garnish

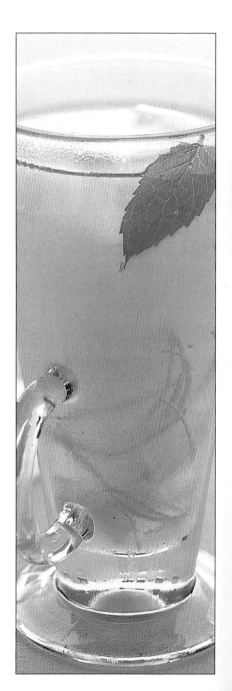

1 Remove the peel from the orange using a vegetable peeler, avoiding the white pith, and cut into long thin strips. Place half the peel and the tea leaves in a bowl and pour in 2 cups (500 ml) boiling water. Cover and leave to steep for 5 minutes, then strain through a fine strainer.
2 Pour into a jug, add the ginger beer and chill for 6 hours, or preferably overnight.
3 One hour before serving, add the ginger, sugar and remaining orange peel. Stir well.
4 Pour into tall glasses, add 2–3 ice cubes per glass and garnish with mint leaves.

NUTRITION: Protein 0 g; Fat 0 g; Carbohydrate 35 g; Dietary Fibre 0 g; Cholesterol 0 g; 585 kJ (140 cal)

LEMON BARLEY WATER

Preparation time: 10 minutes
+ cooling time
Total cooking time: 30 minutes
Makes 4 x 250 ml glasses

1/2 cup (110 g) pearl barley
3 lemons
1/2 cup (125 g) caster sugar
crushed ice, to serve
lemon slices, to garnish

1 Wash the barley well and place in a medium pan. Using a sharp vegetable peeler, remove the peel from the lemons, avoiding the bitter white pith. Squeeze out the juice and set aside. Add the peel and 1.75 litres cold water to the barley and bring to the boil. Simmer briskly for 30 minutes. Add the sugar and mix well to dissolve. Allow to cool.
2 Strain the liquid into a jug and add the lemon juice. Serve over crushed ice and garnish with lemon slices.

NUTRITION: Protein 2.5 g; Fat 0.75 g; Carbohydrate 50 g; Dietary Fibre 4.5 g; Cholesterol 0 g; 890 kJ (210 cal)

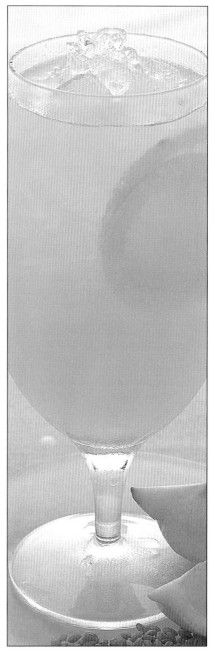

ISLAND SHAKE
Preparation time: 10 minutes
  + chilling time
Makes 2 x 350 ml glasses

400 g fresh mango pulp
1/2 cup (125 ml) fresh lime juice
1/2 cup (125 ml) coconut milk
2 teaspoons honey
3 teaspoons finely chopped fresh mint
200 g ice cubes

1 Place the mango pulp, lime juice, coconut milk, honey, mint and ice in a blender and blend until smooth.
2 Chill well and serve.

NUTRITION: Protein 3.5 g; Fat 13 g; Carbohydrate 34 g; Dietary Fibre 4 g; Cholesterol 0 g; 1120 kJ (270 cal)

FRUIT SPRITZER
Preparation time: 5 minutes
Makes 4 x 375 ml glasses

2 cups (500 ml) apricot nectar, chilled
2 cups (500 ml) soda water, chilled
1 cup (250 ml) apple juice, chilled
1 cup (250 ml) orange juice, chilled
8 ice cubes

1 Place the apricot nectar, soda water, apple juice, orange juice and ice cubes in a large jug and stir until combined.
2 Pour into glasses and serve.

NUTRITION: Protein 0.5 g; Fat 0.2 g; Carbohydrate 30 g; Dietary Fibre 0 g; Cholesterol 0 g; 504 kJ (120 cal)

ICED HONEYED COFFEE
Preparation time: 10 minutes
  + chilling + freezing time
Makes 2 x 375 ml glasses

1 1/2 cups (375 ml) very strong
  (double strength) fresh coffee
2 tablespoons honey
1 1/2 cups (375 ml) milk
caster sugar, to taste

1 Pour the hot coffee into a heatproof jug and add the honey. Stir until the honey has totally dissolved, then chill in the refrigerator.
2 Add the milk and taste for sweetness. Add a little caster sugar if necessary. Pour about 1/2 cup (125 ml) of the mixture into eight holes of an ice cube tray and freeze. Meanwhile, chill the remaining mixture in the refrigerator.
3 When ready to serve, place four coffee ice cubes in each glass, then pour in the iced coffee.

NUTRITION: Protein 7 g; Fat 7.5 g; Carbohydrate 32 g; Dietary Fibre 0.5 g; Cholesterol 25 g; 905 kJ (216 cal)

Note: You can make this using instant coffee, just use twice as many granules as you would for a normal cup of coffee.

Iced Honeyed Coffee (top), Island Shake (left), Fruit Spritzer (right).

ICE CUBES

No more dreary ice cubes—these ideas will bring life to the most humble of drinks!

PASSIONFRUIT AND MINT

Halve 8 passionfruit and divide the seeds and pulp among the ice cube holes. Place a mint leaf on top of each and fill with water. Freeze. Delicious in pineapple juice.

APPLE AND KIWI

Peel and cut 4 kiwi fruit each into eight wedges. Place 1 tablespoon apple juice into each ice cube hole and 2 wedges of kiwi fruit. Freeze. Try this with ginger beer.

STRAWBERRY

Halve 16 strawberries and place 2 halves into each ice cube hole. Top with 1 tablespoon water. Freeze. Great in punches and cocktails.

PINEAPPLE AND PEAR

Divide 1 cup (250 ml) pineapple juice among ice cube holes. Chop 1 unpeeled pear into pieces and place evenly into each hole. Freeze. Serve with apricot nectar.

LEMON, LIME AND BITTERS

Combine $^1\!/_2$ cup (125 ml) lemon juice and $^1\!/_2$ cup (125 ml) lime juice and divide among the ice cube holes. Add 4 drops of bitters to each hole and submerge a lime zest. Freeze. Serve in soda water.

ORANGE AND MANGO

Pour 1 tablespoon freshly squeezed orange juice into each ice cube hole, then divide pieces from 1 mango among the tray, making sure each piece is submerged. Freeze. Delicious in apple juice or soda water.

GINGER ALE AND CUCUMBER

Divide 1 cup (250 ml) ginger ale evenly among ice cube holes. Cut 36 thin slices from a Lebanese cucumber. Place 2 slices of cucumber in each hole. Freeze. Gives a new twist to apple juice.

BERRY AND MINT

Purée 150 g blueberries and 150 g raspberries until smooth, then sieve. Divide among ice cube holes. Top each hole with a mint leaf. Freeze. Great in apple juice and soda water.

HOMEMADE LEMONADE

Preparation time: 20 minutes
  + chilling time
Makes 6 x 375 ml glasses

2³/₄ cups (685 ml) lemon juice
1¹/₄ cups (310 g) sugar
ice cubes, to serve
mint leaves, to garnish

1 Combine the lemon juice and sugar in a large bowl, stirring until the sugar has dissolved. Pour into a large jug.
2 Add 1.25 litres water to the jug, stirring well to combine. Chill.
3 To serve, pour over ice cubes and garnish with mint leaves.

NUTRITION: Protein 0.5 g; Fat 0 g;
Carbohydrate 55 g; Dietary Fibre 0 g;
Cholesterol 0 g; 955 kJ (230 cal)

BANANA PASSION

Preparation time: 5 minutes
Makes 2 x 250 ml glasses

3 passionfruit, halved
1 large banana, chopped
1 cup (250 ml) skim milk
¹/₄ cup (60 g) low-fat plain yoghurt

1 Scoop out the passionfruit pulp and place in a blender. Add the banana, milk and yoghurt and blend, turning quickly on and off (or use the pulse button), until smooth and the seeds are finely chopped. (Add more milk if it is too thick.) Don't blend for too long or it will become very bubbly and increase in volume.

NUTRITION: Protein 8.5 g; Fat 0.5 g;
Carbohydrate 25 g; Dietary Fibre 5.5 g;
Cholesterol 5.5 g; 565 kJ (135 cal)

SMOOTHBERRY
Preparation time: 5 minutes
 + chilling time
Makes 4 x 200 ml glasses

150 g strawberries, hulled
60 g raspberries
200 g boysenberries
1 cup (250 ml) milk
3 scoops vanilla ice cream

1 Place the strawberries,
raspberries, boysenberries, milk
and ice cream in a blender and
blend until smooth. Chill.
2 Pour into glasses and serve.

NUTRITION: Protein 4 g; Fat 5 g;
Carbohydrate 12 g; Dietary Fibre 4.5 g;
Cholesterol 13 g; 450 kJ (107 cal)

Note: If boysenberries are unavailable, any
other berry can be used.

ICED CHOCOLATE
Preparation time: 5 minutes
Makes 1 x 375 ml glass

2 tablespoons rich chocolate topping
1 1/2 cups (375 ml) icy-cold milk
1 scoop vanilla ice cream
whipped cream, to serve
drinking chocolate, to serve

1 Pour the chocolate topping into
a glass and swirl it around the
sides. Fill with the cold milk and
add the ice cream.
2 Serve with a big swirl of whipped
cream and dust with drinking
chocolate.

NUTRITION: Protein 14 g; Fat 26 g;
Carbohydrate 45 g; Dietary Fibre 0 g;
Cholesterol 85 g; 1902 kJ (455 cal)

LEMON GRASS TEA

Preparation time: 5 minutes
  + cooling + chilling time
Makes 2 x 310 ml

3 lemon grass stalks
2 slices lemon
3 teaspoons honey, or to taste
lemon slices, extra, to serve

1 Prepare the lemon grass by removing the first two tough outer layers. For maximum flavour, only use the bottom one-third of the stalk (the white part). Slice thinly into rings. (You could use the remaining stalks as a garnish, if you like.)

2 Place the lemon grass in a jug and cover with 2½ cups (625 ml) boiling water. Add the lemon slices and cover. Allow to infuse and cool. When cooled to room temperature, strain. Add the honey, to taste. Place the tea in the refrigerator to chill.

3 To serve, pour the tea into two glasses with extra slices of lemon. Add ice, if desired.

NUTRITION: Protein 0 g; Fat 0 g; Carbohydrate 8.5 g; Dietary Fibre 0.25 g; Cholesterol 0 g; 145 kJ (35 cal)

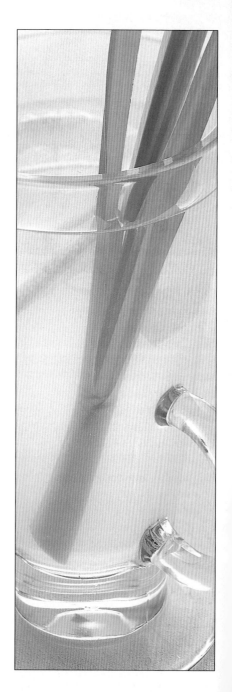

RASPBERRY LEMONADE

Preparation time: 20 minutes
+ chilling time
Makes 6 x 375 ml glasses

300 g fresh or frozen raspberries,
  thawed
1¼ cups (310 g) sugar
2 cups (500 ml) lemon juice
ice cubes, to serve
mint leaves, to garnish

1 Combine the raspberries and sugar in a blender and blend until smooth.
2 Place a strong sieve over a large bowl and push the mixture through to remove the seeds. Discard the seeds.
3 Add the lemon juice and mix well. Pour into a large jug and stir in 1.5 litres water, then refrigerate until cold.
4 To serve, pour over ice cubes and garnish with mint leaves.

NUTRITION: Protein 0.8 g; Fat 0.3 g;
Carbohydrate 50 g; Dietary Fibre 2.5 g;
Cholesterol 0 g; 855 kJ (205 cal)

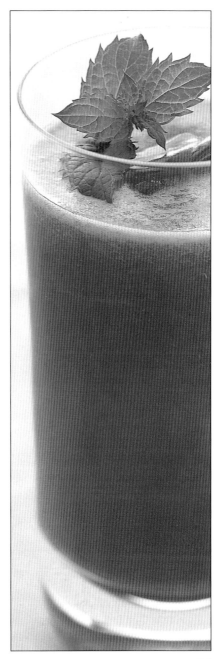

RASPBERRY AND APPLE JUICE

Preparation time: 5 minutes
  + chilling time
Makes 2 x 375 ml glasses

6 Granny Smith apples, quartered
150 g fresh raspberries
ice cubes, to serve
mint sprigs, to garnish

1 Using the plunger, push the apple pieces and raspberries through a juicer and into a jug. Chill.
2 Stir well before serving. Add ice and garnish with mint sprigs.

NUTRITION: Protein 1.5 g; Fat 0.5 g; Carbohydrate 30 g; Dietary Fibre 8 g; Cholesterol 0 g; 515 kJ (125 cal)

HAWAIIAN CRUSH

Preparation time: 10 minutes
  + chilling time
Makes 2 x 375 ml glasses

1 cup (250 ml) apple juice
100 g papaya, peeled, seeded, chopped
200 g watermelon, seeded, chopped
100 g ice cubes

1 Blend the apple juice, papaya, watermelon and ice cubes in a blender until smooth. Chill well.
2 Pour into glasses and serve.

NUTRITION: Protein 0.8 g; Fat 0.3 g; Carbohydrate 25 g; Dietary Fibre 1.35 g; Cholesterol 0 g; 420 kJ (100 cal)

ICED LEMON AND PEPPERMINT TEA

Preparation time: 10 minutes
  + infusing + chilling time
Makes 2 x 375 ml glasses

2 peppermint tea bags
6 strips lemon rind (2 x 5 cm)
1 tablespoon sugar (or to taste)
ice cubes, to serve
mint leaves, to garnish

1 Place the tea bags and lemon rind strips in a large bowl. Cover with $3^1/_3$ cups (830 ml) boiling water and leave to infuse for 5 minutes.
2 Squeeze out the tea bags and discard. Stir in the sugar to taste.
3 Pour into a jug and chill. Serve in chilled glasses with ice cubes and mint leaves.

NUTRITION: Protein 0 g; Fat 0 g; Carbohydrate 10 g; Dietary Fibre 0 g; Cholesterol 0 g; 165 kJ (40 cal)

Note: For a different idea, pour about $^1/_2$ cup (125 ml) of the tea mixture into 8 holes of an ice cube tray. Freeze and serve with the chilled tea.

Iced Lemon and Peppermint Tea (top), Raspberry and Apple Juice (left), Hawaiian Crush (right).

FENNEL AND ORANGE JUICE

Preparation time: 10 minutes
  + chilling time
Makes 2 x 375 ml glasses

8 oranges
150 g baby fennel

1 Peel and quarter the oranges, and remove any seeds. Trim the fennel and cut in half.
2 Using a juicer, push the fennel through first to release the flavours, then juice the orange. Chill well.
3 Mix together well before serving.

NUTRITION: Protein 5.5 g; Fat 0.5 g; Carbohydrate 40 g; Dietary Fibre 12 g; Cholesterol 0 g; 820 kJ (195 cal)

Note: When in season, the flavour will be stronger in larger, more developed fennel.

TOO GOOD FOR YOU

Preparation time: 15 minutes
Makes 4 x 200 ml glasses

1 large apple, cored
6 carrots, tops removed
4 celery sticks, including leaves
6 iceberg lettuce leaves
20 English spinach leaves

1 Cut the apple, carrots and celery sticks to fit the juicer.
2 Using the plunger, push all the ingredients through the juicer and into a large jug.
3 Pour into glasses and serve with ice, if desired.

NUTRITION: Protein 2.5 g; Fat 0.32 g; Carbohydrate 12 g; Dietary Fibre 7 g; Cholesterol 0 g; 248 kJ (59 cal)

GREEN PUNCH

Preparation time: 15 minutes
Makes 2 x 250 ml glasses

1 green apple, cored
1/2 medium honeydew melon, peeled,
    seeds removed
2 oranges, peeled
ice cubes, to serve

1 Cut the apple, melon and oranges into pieces to fit the juicer.
2 Using the plunger, push all the ingredients through the juicer and into a jug.
3 Pour into glasses and serve with ice.

NUTRITION: Protein 2 g; Fat 0.5 g; Carbohydrate 25 g; Dietary Fibre 5 g; Cholesterol 0 g; 465 kJ (110 cal)

CELERY, TOMATO AND PARSLEY JUICE

Preparation time: 5 minutes
    + chilling time
Makes 2 x 400 ml glasses

1 cup (15 g) fresh parsley
6 vine-ripened tomatoes, quartered
4 celery sticks, trimmed

1 Using a juicer, push through the parsley leaves to infuse the flavour. Then juice the tomatoes and celery. Chill well.
2 Before serving, mix together well and garnish with a stick of celery as a swizzle stick.

NUTRITION: Protein 4.5 g; Fat 0.5 g; Carbohydrate 8.5 g; Dietary Fibre 6 g; Cholesterol 0 g; 245 kJ (60 cal)

Note: For extra spice, add a few drops of Tabasco and freshly ground black pepper.

PINEAPPLE AND COCONUT ICED DRINK

Preparation time: 10 minutes
    + freezing + chilling time
Makes 2 x 375 ml glasses

2 cups (500 ml) fresh pineapple juice
I cup (250 ml) coconut milk
mint leaves, to garnish
pineapple leaves, to garnish

1 Combine the pineapple juice with the coconut milk in a large jug and mix well. Pour ¹/₂ cup (125 ml) of the mixture into 8 holes of an ice cube tray and freeze. Chill the remaining mixture in the refrigerator.
2 When the the ice cubes have frozen, pour the chilled juice mixture into 2 glasses, add the frozen cubes and garnish with mint and pineapple leaves.

NUTRITION: Protein 3.5 g; Fat 25 g; Carbohydrate 30 g; Dietary Fibre 6 g; Cholesterol 0 g; 1520 kJ (365 cal)

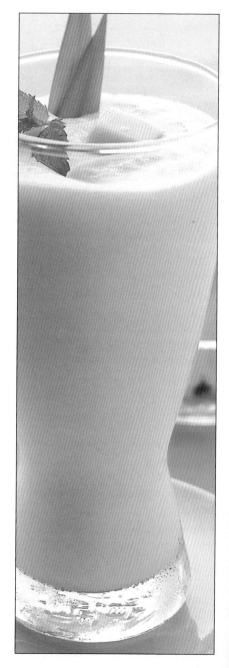

PAPAYA AND ORANGE SMOOTHIE
Preparation time: 10 minutes
Makes 2 x 300 ml glasses

1 medium (650 g) papaya
1 medium orange
6–8 ice cubes
200 g plain yoghurt
1–2 tablespoons caster sugar
ground nutmeg, to garnish

1 Peel the papaya and remove the seeds. Cut the flesh into cubes. Peel the orange and roughly chop the flesh.
2 Place the papaya, orange and ice in a blender and blend until smooth. Blend in the yoghurt, and add sugar, to taste.
3 Divide between two glasses, sprinkle lightly with nutmeg and serve.

NUTRITION: Protein 8.5 g; Fat 4 g; Carbohydrate 70 g; Dietary Fibre 6 g; Cholesterol 16 g; 1485 kJ (355 cal)

Note: This keeps well for 6 hours in the fridge and is best in both flavour and colour when the small Fijian papaya are used. Peach or apricot flavoured yoghurt may be used for added flavour.

BLUEBERRY STARTER
Preparation time: 10 minutes
Makes 2 x 375 ml glasses

200 g fresh or frozen blueberries
1 cup (250 g) plain yoghurt
1 cup (250 ml) milk
1 tablespoon wheat germ
1–2 teaspoons honey, or to taste

1 Blend together the blueberries, yoghurt, milk, wheat germ and honey until smooth.
2 Pour into glasses and serve immediately.

NUTRITION: Protein 13 g; Fat 10 g; Carbohydrate 30 g; Dietary Fibre 3.5 g; Cholesterol 35 g; 1135 kJ (270 cal)

Note: Frozen blueberries are great for this recipe. No need to thaw, just throw into the blender frozen!

SPORTS SHAKE
Preparation time: 5 minutes
  + chilling time
Makes 2 x 250 ml glasses

2 cups (500 ml) milk, chilled
2 tablespoons honey
2 eggs
1/2 teaspoon vanilla essence
1 tablespoon wheat germ
1 medium banana, sliced

1 Blend the milk, honey, eggs, vanilla, wheat germ and banana until smooth.
2 Chill well and serve.

NUTRITION: Protein 15 g; Fat 15 g; Carbohydrate 45 g; Dietary Fibre 2 g; Cholesterol 215 g; 1585 kJ (380 cal)

DINNER IN A GLASS
Preparation time: 10 minutes
Makes 2 x 400 ml glasses

10–12 medium carrots
1 medium beetroot
2 medium green apples
2 English spinach leaves
2 celery sticks

1 Cut the carrots to fit the juicer.
2 Scrub the beetroot to ensure all the dirt is removed. Cut the beetroot and apples to fit the juicer.
3 Using the plunger, push all the ingredients through the juicer and into a large jug.
4 Serve chilled or over ice.

NUTRITION: Protein 6 g; Fat 0 g; Carbohydrate 50 g; Dietary Fibre 22 g; Cholesterol 0 g; 930 kJ (222 cal)

WATERMELON BREAKFAST JUICE
Preparation time: 10 minutes
Makes 2 x 400 ml glasses

4 cups (720 g) chopped watermelon, seeded
2 tablespoons lime juice
1–2 cm fresh ginger, grated, to taste
2 tablespoons chopped fresh mint

1 Blend the watermelon, lime juice, ginger and mint in a blender using the pulse button (or by quickly turning the blender on and off a number of times). Be careful not to overblend or the mixture will go frothy.
2 Divide between two glasses.

NUTRITION: Protein 1 g; Fat 0.5 g; Carbohydrate 18 g; Dietary Fibre 2 g; Cholesterol 0 g; 355 kJ (85 cal)

ICED MINT TEA

Preparation time: 5 minutes
 + cooling + chilling time
Makes 6 x 250 ml glasses

4 peppermint tea bags
¹/₃ cup (115 ml) honey
2 cups (500 ml) grapefruit juice
1 cup (250 ml) orange juice
mint sprigs, to garnish

1 Place the tea bags in a large
heatproof jug and pour in 3 cups
(750 ml) boiling water. Allow to
steep for 3 minutes, then remove
and discard the bags. Stir in the
honey and allow to cool.
2 Add the grapefruit and orange
juice. Cover and chill in the
refrigerator. Serve in glasses,
garnished with fresh mint.

NUTRITION: Protein 0.3 g; Fat 0 g;
Carbohydrate 30 g; Dietary Fibre 0 g;
Cholesterol 0 g; 510 kJ (122 cal)

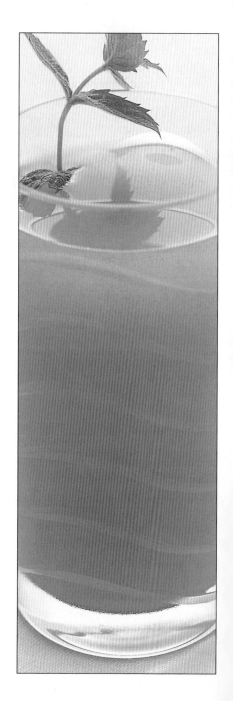

SPRING CLEAN YOUR BODY

Preparation time: 10 minutes
Makes 4 x 250 ml glasses

2 large cucumbers
6 medium (600 g) carrots
I large green apple
2 celery sticks, including leaves
I large beetroot

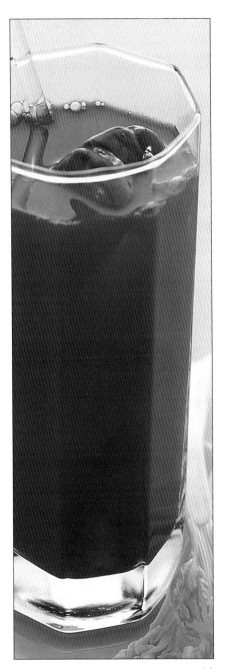

1 Remove the skin from the cucumbers. Cut the cucumbers, carrots, apple and celery into pieces to fit the juicer.
2 Scrub the beetroot with a firm brush to remove any dirt and cut to fit the juicer.
3 Using the plunger, push the fruit and vegetables through the juicer into a large jug.
4 Serve chilled or with ice.

NUTRITION: Protein 2 g; Fat 0 g;
Carbohydrate 16 g; Dietary Fibre 7 g;
Cholesterol 0 g; 310 kJ (75 cal)

PEANUT CHOC POWER
Preparation time: 15 minutes
Makes 4 x 250 ml glasses

2 cups (500 ml) chocolate-flavoured
   soy milk, chilled
125 g soft silken tofu
1/4 cup (60 g) smooth peanut butter
2 bananas, sliced
2 tablespoons chocolate syrup
8 large ice cubes

1 Combine the soy milk, tofu and
peanut butter in a blender.
2 Add the banana, chocolate syrup
and ice cubes. Blend until smooth.

NUTRITION: Protein 11 g; Fat 15 g;
Carbohydrate 27 g; Dietary Fibre 4 g;
Cholesterol 0 g; 463 kJ (110 cal)

PEAR, APPLE AND GINGER JUICE
Preparation time: 5 minutes
Makes 2 x 375 ml glasses

3 cm piece fresh ginger
3 ripe pears, cored, quartered, chilled
5 Granny Smith apples, quartered, chilled

1 Using a juicer, juice the ginger,
pear and apple together. Pour
into a jug.
2 Mix together well and serve
immediately.

NUTRITION: Protein 2 g; Fat 0.5 g;
Carbohydrate 75 g; Dietary Fibre 13 g;
Cholesterol 0 g; 1255 kJ (300 cal)

Note: Ensure the fruit is well chilled before
juicing as this drink should be served
immediately—separation of flavours occurs
quickly and the fruit will discolour.

MIXED BERRY AND LEMONADE FIZZ
Preparation time: 10 minutes
Makes 4 x 250 ml glasses

50 g fresh blueberries
100 g fresh strawberries, hulled
3 cups (750 ml) lemonade
2 scoops lemon sorbet

1 Place the berries, lemonade and lemon sorbet into a blender and purée until well combined.
2 Pour into cold glasses and serve immediately with extra berries, if desired.

NUTRITION: Protein 1 g; Fat 0.5 g; Carbohydrate 23 g; Dietary Fibre 1 g; Cholesterol 1.32 g; 397 kJ (95 cal)

Note: Any berries can be used. Use frozen or any fresh berries that are in season.

PINEAPPLE KICK
Preparation time: 10 minutes
Makes 2 x 250 ml glasses

3 oranges, peeled
600 g chopped fresh pineapple
3 1/2 cm piece fresh ginger

1 Cut the oranges into pieces to fit the juicer.
2 Using the plunger, push the orange pieces, pineapple and ginger through the juicer and into a jug.
3 Pour into glasses and serve with ice.

NUTRITION: Protein 5 g; Fat 0.5 g; Carbohydrate 40 g; Dietary Fibre 10 g; Cholesterol 0 g; 770 kJ (185 cal)

MILK SHAKES
Old favourites that will never disappear from the café menu.

DOUBLE CHOCOLATE SHAKE
Blend 1 cup (250 ml) cold chocolate milk and 4 scoops chocolate ice cream in a blender until smooth. Pour into chilled glasses and decorate with grated chocolate.
Makes 2 x 250 ml glasses.

CARAMEL SHAKE
Blend 1 cup (250 ml) cold milk, 2 scoops vanilla ice cream and $\frac{1}{4}$ cup (60 ml) caramel fudge sauce in a blender until smooth. Pour into chilled glasses.
Makes 2 x 250 ml glasses.

STRAWBERRY SHAKE
Blend 1 tablespoon strawberry
flavouring, $^2/_3$ cup (170 ml) cold
milk, $^1/_3$ cup (80 ml) cream and
2 scoops strawberry ice cream in a
blender until smooth. Serve in
chilled glasses.
Makes 2 x 250 ml glasses.

MALTED VANILLA SHAKE
Blend 1 cup (250 ml) cold milk,
2 tablespoons malt powder and
4 scoops vanilla ice cream in a
blender until smooth. Taste, then add
sugar if desired. Pour into chilled
glasses and decorate with a sprinkle
of drinking chocolate.
Makes 2 x 250 ml glasses.

YOGHURT AND HONEY SMOOTHIE

Preparation time: 10 minutes
Makes 4 x 250 ml glasses

I cup (250 g) thick plain yoghurt
3 tablespoons honey
I cup (250 ml) milk
3 scoops vanilla ice cream

1 Blend the yoghurt and honey in a blender for 10 seconds, or until well combined. Add the milk and ice cream and blend until smooth.
2 Serve in chilled glasses.

NUTRITION: Protein 6 g; Fat 6.5 g; Carbohydrate 26 g; Dietary Fibre 0 g; Cholesterol 23 g; 777 kJ (186 cal)

ORANGE ICE CREAM SODA

Preparation time: 10 minutes
Makes 2 x 375 ml glasses

2 cups (500 ml) freshly squeezed orange juice
I cup (250 ml) lemonade
2–4 scoops lemon sorbet

1 Combine the orange juice and lemonade in a jug. Pour into large chilled glasses, allowing enough room for the sorbet.
2 Add 1–2 scoops sorbet per glass.

NUTRITION: Protein 1.5 g; Fat 3.5 g; Carbohydrate 47 g; Dietary Fibre 0 g; Cholesterol 6.5 g; 925 kJ (220 cal)

SUMMER DE-TOX

Preparation time: 15 minutes
Makes 2 x 375 ml glasses

3 oranges
250 g fresh strawberries
300 g seedless grapes
2 peaches

1 Peel the oranges and cut to fit the juicer. Push through with the plunger.
2 Wash and hull the strawberries. Push the strawberries and grapes through the juicer with the plunger.
3 Place the peaches in a heatproof bowl and cover with boiling water. Leave for 30 seconds, then transfer to cold water. Peel away the skin. Cut the flesh from the stone and push through the juicer with the plunger.
4 Pour into each glass and serve with long spoons.

NUTRITION: Protein 5.5 g; Fat 0.5 g; Carbohydrate 45 g; Dietary Fibre 9 g; Cholesterol 0 g; 885 kJ (212 cal)

Summer De-tox (top), **Yoghurt and Honey Smoothie** (left), **Orange Ice Cream Soda** (right).

PASSIONFRUIT ICE CREAM SODA

Preparation time: 10 minutes
Makes 2 x 375 ml glasses

6 passionfruit, halved
2¹/₂ cups (625 ml) lemonade
2–4 scoops vanilla ice cream

1 Scoop out the passionfruit pulp into a jug—there should be about ¹/₂ cup (125 g). Combine the pulp with the lemonade and pour into 2 large chilled glasses—allow enough room for the ice cream.
2 Add 1–2 scoops of ice cream to each glass and serve with straws and long spoons.

NUTRITION: Protein 4 g; Fat 5.5 g; Carbohydrate 45 g; Dietary Fibre 8.5 g; Cholesterol 13 g; 1030 kJ (250 cal)

MORNING BLENDED FRUIT JUICE

Preparation time: 10 minutes
Makes 4 x 300 ml glasses

¹/₂ fresh pineapple, peeled and cored
1¹/₂ cups (375 ml) fresh orange juice
1 large pear, chopped
1 banana, chopped
40 g chopped pawpaw

1 Chop the pineapple flesh into pieces and place in the blender. Add the orange juice, pear, banana and pawpaw and blend together until smooth.
2 Serve immediately.

NUTRITION: Protein 1.5 g; Fat 0.5 g; Carbohydrate 27 g; Dietary Fibre 4 g; Cholesterol 0 g; 500 kJ (120 cal)

BREAKFAST SHAKE

Preparation time: 10 minutes
Makes 2 x 325 ml glasses

150 g fruit (passionfruit, mango, banana,
   peaches, strawberries, blueberries)
1 cup (250 ml) milk
2 teaspoons wheat germ
1 tablespoon honey
1/4 cup (60 g) vanilla yoghurt
1 egg, optional
1 tablespoon malt powder

1 Blend all the ingredients in
a blender for 30–60 seconds, or
until well combined.
2 Pour into chilled glasses and
serve immediately.

NUTRITION: Protein 20 g; Fat 12 g;
Carbohydrate 35 g; Dietary Fibre 7 g;
Cholesterol 115 g; 1320 kJ (315 cal)

AMERICAN ICED TEA

Preparation time: 10 minutes
   + cooling + chilling time
Makes 8 x 250 ml glasses

4 Ceylon tea bags
2 tablespoons sugar
2 tablespoons lemon juice
1 1/2 cups (375 ml) dark grape juice
2 cups (500 ml) orange juice
1 1/2 cups (375 ml) ginger ale
lemon slices, to serve

1 Place the tea bags in a heatproof
bowl with 1 litre boiling water.
Leave for 3 minutes. Remove the
bags and stir in the sugar. Cool.
2 Stir in the juices. Refrigerate until
cold, then add the ginger ale. Serve
over ice cubes with a slice of lemon.

NUTRITION: Protein 0 g; Fat 0 g;
Carbohydrate 25 g; Dietary Fibre 0 g;
Cholesterol 0 g; 400 kJ (45 cal)

HONEYDEW MELON
AND PASSIONFRUIT

Preparation time: 10 minutes
  + chilling time
Makes 2 x 375 ml glasses

750 g honeydew melon
  (about 1 whole medium fruit)
6 passionfruit (see Note)
ice cubes, to serve

1 Peel and seed the melon. Cut into pieces to fit the juicer.
2 Halve the passionfruit and scoop out the pulp.
3 Feed the melon pieces through the juicer and stir through the passionfruit pulp. Chill well.
4 Serve in a jug with lots of ice.

NUTRITION: Protein 4.5 g; Fat 1 g;
Carbohydrate 28 g; Dietary Fibre 13 g;
Cholesterol 0 g; 615 kJ (145 cal)

Note: The amount of passionfruit pulp depends on the fruit. If the passionfruit are not juicy use one 120 g can passionfruit pulp.

GREEN APPLE AND LEMON THIRST QUENCHER

Preparation time: 10 minutes
Makes 2 x 350 ml glasses

1/3 cup (80 ml) lemon juice, chilled
6 medium (1 kg) green apples, chilled
mint leaves, to garnish

1 Pour the lemon juice into the serving jug.
2 Wash the apples and cut into smaller pieces to fit into the juicer. Using the plunger, push the apples through the juicer.
3 Add the apple juice to the lemon juice and stir well. Garnish with mint leaves and serve immediately.

NUTRITION: Protein 1.5 g; Fat 0.5 g; Carbohydrate 60 g; Dietary Fibre 10 g; Cholesterol 0 g; 1080 kJ (260 cal)

Note: This is a refreshing, slightly tart drink. If the apples and lemons are not cold, throw a handful of ice cubes into the blender and pulse.

HONEYCOMB SMOOTHIE
Preparation time: 5 minutes
Makes 2 x 375 ml glasses

1¹/₄ cups (315 ml) cold milk
¹/₂ cup (125 g) plain Greek-style
  yoghurt
2 teaspoons honey
70 g chocolate honeycomb bar,
  roughly chopped
3 scoops vanilla ice cream

1 Blend all the ingredients in
a blender until smooth.
2 Serve immediately.

NUTRITION: Protein 11 g; Fat 18 g;
Carbohydrate 48 g; Dietary Fibre 0 g;
Cholesterol 40 g; 1620 kJ (387 cal)

APPLE AND
BLACKCURRANT SHAKE
Preparation time: 5 minutes
Makes 2 x 375 ml glasses

1 cup (250 ml) apple and
  blackcurrant juice
³/₄ cup (185 ml) milk
2 tablespoons plain yoghurt
3 scoops vanilla ice cream

1 Blend the juice, milk, yoghurt
and ice cream in a blender until
well combined and fluffy.
2 Serve immediately.

NUTRITION: Protein 9.5 g; Fat 12 g;
Carbohydrate 45 g; Dietary Fibre 0 g;
Cholesterol 40 g; 1360 kJ (325 cal)

LAVENDER AND
ROSE LEMONADE
Preparation time: 5 minutes
  + infusing + chilling time
Makes 6 x 250 ml glasses

2 lemons
15 g lavender flowers (stripped
  from their stems)
¹/₂ cup (125 g) sugar
¹/₂ teaspoon rosewater

1 Using a sharp vegetable peeler,
remove the peel from the lemons,
avoiding the bitter white pith.
Squeeze the juice and set aside.
Place the lemon peel in a
heatproof jug with the lavender
flowers and sugar and pour in
2 cups (500 ml) boiling water.
Mix well.
2 Cover with plastic wrap and
leave for 15 minutes. Strain,
then add the lemon juice and
the rosewater. Add enough cold
water to make 1.5 litres. Serve
well chilled. Garnish with fresh
edible rose petals, if you wish.

NUTRITION: Protein 0 g; Fat 0 g;
Carbohydrate 20 g; Dietary Fibre 1 g;
Cholesterol 0 g; 332 kJ (80 cal)

Note: Rosewater is available in good
supermarkets, delicatessans and
speciality shops.

Lavender and Rose Lemonade (top),
Honeycomb Smoothie (left), Apple and
Blackcurrant Shake (right).

PUNCHES

Great for entertaining, self-serve punches quench the thirst of a mingling crowd.

PINEAPPLE AND PAWPAW JUICE

Peel a 2 kg fresh pineapple and remove the centre core. Roughly chop the flesh. Juice the pineapple in a juicer and place in a blender with 600 g pawpaw. Blend until smooth. Add 1 cup (250 ml) chilled ginger ale and pour into chilled glasses. Serve immediately. Garnish with extra slices of pineapple.

Makes 4 x 250 ml glasses

SPARKLING PUNCH

Place 1 cup (250 ml) pineapple juice, 2 cups (500 ml) orange juice, 2 cups (500 ml) apple cider and 2 cups (500 ml) ginger ale in a jug and stir. Scoop out the flesh from 2 passionfruit and stir into the juice. Garnish with 2 slices orange, halved and 2 slices lemon, halved.

Makes 6 x 250 ml glasses

PINEAPPLE DELIGHT

Peel a 750 g fresh pineapple and remove the centre core. Cut the flesh into 2 cm pieces and blend in a blender for 1–2 minutes, or until as smooth as possible. Pour 2 cups (500 ml) lemonade into a jug and add the pineapple purée, stirring gently to combine. Add 2 tablespoons lime juice and mix well. Pour into the serving glasses and garnish with mint leaves.

Makes 4 x 250 ml glasses

BERRY AND CHERRY PUNCH

Using a vegetable peeler, remove the skin from 1 lemon, avoiding the bitter white pith. Cut into long thin strips. Remove the stones from 375 g cherries and place the cherries in a jug. Add 200 g blackberries, 200 g blueberries, 125 g strawberries, halved, 3 cups (750 ml) ginger ale, 2 cups (500 ml) lemonade, 1 cup (250 ml) cold black tea, the lemon rind and 10 coarsely torn mint leaves. Cover the jug and chill for at least 3 hours. Add ice cubes to serve.

Makes 10 x 250 ml glasses

CINNAMON AND CUSTARD SHAKE

Preparation time: 5 minutes
Makes 2 x 375 ml glasses

1¹/₂ cups (375 ml) milk
³/₄ cup (185 ml) prepared custard
3 teaspoons honey
1¹/₂ teaspoons ground cinnamon
3 scoops vanilla ice cream
ground cinnamon, extra, to serve

1 Blend together the milk, custard, honey, cinnamon and ice cream until smooth and fluffy.
2 Pour into tall glasses, sprinkle with extra cinnamon and serve immediately.

NUTRITION: Protein 10 g; Fat 15 g; Carbohydrate 35 g; Dietary Fibre 0 g; Cholesterol 45 g; 1280 kJ (305 cal)

CHOC CHERRY SMOOTHIE

Preparation time: 5 minutes
Makes 2 x 375 ml glasses

2 cups (500 ml) milk
¹/₄ cup (55 g) whole red glacé cherries
¹/₄ cup (25 g) desiccated coconut
1 tablespoon chocolate topping
3 scoops chocolate ice cream

1 Blend together the milk, cherries, coconut, topping and ice cream until smooth and fluffy.
2 Pour into tall glasses and serve immediately.

NUTRITION: Protein 11 g; Fat 22 g; Carbohydrate 44 g; Dietary Fibre 2 g; Cholesterol 44 g; 1700 kJ (405 cal)

CHOC CARAMEL SMOOTHIE

Preparation time: 5 minutes
Makes 2 x 325 ml glasses

1¹/₂ cups (375 ml) cold milk
100 g chocolate-covered caramel
  nougat bar, roughly chopped
2 teaspoons chocolate topping
4 scoops chocolate ice cream

1 Blend the milk, chocolate bar,
chocolate topping and ice cream
together until smooth.
2 Serve immediately.

NUTRITION: Protein 12 g; Fat 23 g;
Carbohydrate 45 g; Dietary Fibre 2 g;
Cholesterol 40 g; 1804 kJ (430 cal)

Note: There will still be some small pieces
of chocolate after blending.

COCONUT AND PASSIONFRUIT SMOOTHIE

Preparation time: 5 minutes
Makes 2 x 375 ml glasses

140 ml can coconut milk
1 cup (250 ml) milk
¹/₄ cup (25 g) desiccated coconut
¹/₄ teaspoon vanilla essence
3 scoops vanilla ice cream
170 g can passionfruit pulp in syrup

1 Blend together the coconut milk,
milk, coconut, vanilla, ice cream
and half the passionfruit pulp until
smooth and fluffy.
2 Stir in the remaining pulp and
serve immediately.

NUTRITION: Protein 10 g; Fat 30 g;
Carbohydrate 21 g; Dietary Fibre 15 g;
Cholesterol 25 g; 1645 kJ (395 cal)

EARL GREY SUMMER TEA

Preparation time: 10 minutes
  + cooling + chilling time
Makes 4 x 250 ml glasses

1 cinnamon stick
1 tablespoon Earl Grey tea leaves
1 cup (250 ml) orange juice
2 teaspoons finely grated orange rind
2 tablespoons sugar, to taste
ice cubes, to serve
1 orange, sliced into thin rounds
4 cinnamon sticks, extra, to garnish

1 Place the cinnamon stick, tea leaves, orange juice, orange rind and 3 cups (750 ml) water in a medium pan.
2 Slowly bring to a simmer over gentle heat. Once simmering, stir in the sugar, to taste, and stir until dissolved. Remove from the heat and allow to cool. Once the mixture has cooled, strain the liquid into a jug and refrigerate until cold.
3 Serve in a jug with lots of ice cubes, and garnish with the orange slices and extra cinnamon stick.

NUTRITION: Protein 0 g; Fat 0 g;
Carbohydrate 20 g; Dietary Fibre 0 g;
Cholesterol 0 g; 295 kJ (70 cal)

MINT JULEP

Preparation time: 5 minutes
  + infusing + chilling time
Makes 2 x 300 ml glasses

I cup (20 g) fresh mint leaves
I tablespoon sugar
I tablespoon lemon juice
I cup (250 ml) pineapple juice
I cup (250 ml) ginger ale
ice cubes, to serve
mint leaves, to garnish

1 Roughly chop the mint leaves and place in a heatproof jug with the sugar. Using a wooden spoon, bruise the mint. Add the lemon juice, pineapple juice and $1/2$ cup (125 ml) boiling water. Mix well. Cover with plastic wrap and leave for 30 minutes.
2 Strain, then refrigerate until cold.
3 Just before serving, add the ginger ale and mix well. Serve in glasses over ice and garnish with mint leaves.

NUTRITION: Protein 0 g; Fat 0 g; Carbohydrate 22 g; Dietary Fibre 0 g; Cholesterol 0 g; 363 kJ (87 cal)

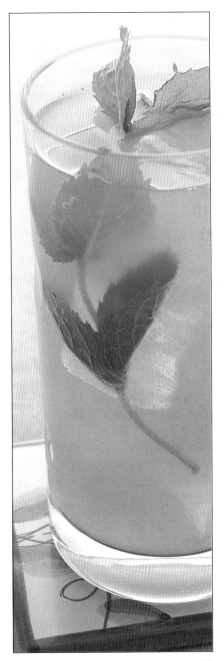

APRICOT TOFU SMOOTHIE

Preparation time: 15 minutes
Makes 2 x 375 ml glasses

4 apricots, halved and stoned
2 peaches, halved and stoned
I cup (250 ml) apricot nectar, chilled
150 g silken tofu

1 Place the apricots, peaches, nectar and tofu in a blender and blend until smooth.
2 Pour into glasses and serve.

NUTRITION: Protein 2 g; Fat 1.5 g; Carbohydrate 30 g; Dietary Fibre 3.5 g; Cholesterol 0 g; 750 kJ (178 cal)

PEAR AND MINT FRAPPE

Preparation time: 15 minutes
Makes 2 x 375 ml glasses

4 ripe pears, peeled and cored
3 teaspoons caster sugar
2 teaspoons roughly chopped fresh mint
30 ice cubes
mint leaves, extra, to garnish

1 Chop the pear flesh into pieces. Place in a blender with the sugar and mint and blend until smooth.
2 Add the ice cubes and blend until smooth.
3 Serve immediately, garnished with the extra mint leaves.

NUTRITION: Protein 1 g; Fat 0 g; Carbohydrate 40 g; Dietary Fibre 6.5 g; Cholesterol 0 g; 640 kJ (155 cal)

DECADENT SWIRLED CHOCOLATE MINT THICKSHAKE

Preparation time: 10 minutes
Makes 4 x 250 ml glasses

I cup (250 ml) milk
1 1/4 tablespoons chocolate syrup
5 scoops chocolate ice cream
35 g chocolate-coated peppermint crisp bar, roughly chopped
I tablespoon chopped fresh mint
5 scoops vanilla ice cream

1 Blend half the milk with the chocolate syrup and chocolate ice cream. Pour into 4 glasses.
2 Blend the peppermint crisp bar with the remaining milk, mint and vanilla ice cream. Pour over the chocolate mixture and swirl together to combine.
3 Serve immediately with a straw.

NUTRITION: Protein 5 g; Fat 15 g; Carbohydrate 25 g; Dietary Fibre 0 g; Cholesterol 0 g; 954 kJ (228 cal)

Decadent Swirled Chocolate Mint Thickshake (top), Apricot Tofu Smoothie (left), Pear and Mint Frappé (right).

COCONUT AND LIME LASSI
Preparation time: 10 minutes
Makes 2 x 375 ml glasses

400 ml coconut milk
3/4 cup (185 g) plain yoghurt
1/4 cup (60 ml) fresh lime juice
1/4 cup (60 g) caster sugar
8–10 ice cubes
lime slices, to garnish

1 Blend together the coconut milk,
yoghurt, lime juice, sugar and ice
cubes until the mixture is well
combined and the ice cubes are
well crushed.
2 Pour into tall glasses and serve
immediately, garnished with slices
of fresh lime.

NUTRITION: Protein 8 g; Fat 45 g;
Carbohydrate 40 g; Dietary Fibre 3.5 g;
Cholesterol 15 g; 2438 kJ (585 cal)

ISLAND BLEND
Preparation time: 15 minutes
Makes 2 x 350 ml glasses

100 g chopped fresh pineapple
1/2 small papaya, seeded and chopped
2 small bananas, sliced
1/4 cup (60 ml) coconut milk
I cup (250 ml) orange juice
ice cubes, to serve

1 Cut the pineapple and papaya
into smaller chunks and place in
a blender. Add the banana and
coconut milk and blend until
smooth. Add the orange juice and
blend until combined.
2 Pour into glasses and serve
with ice.

NUTRITION: Protein 6.5 g; Fat 7 g;
Carbohydrate 85 g; Dietary Fibre 9 g;
Cholesterol 0 g; 1797 kJ (430 cal)

SUMMER STRAWBERRY SMOOTHIE

Preparation time: 10 minutes
Makes 2 x 300 ml glasses

1 tablespoon strawberry flavouring
1 cup (250 ml) wildberry drinking
  yoghurt
250 g strawberries, hulled
4 scoops frozen strawberry yoghurt
few drops vanilla essence
ice cubes, to serve

1 Combine the strawberry
flavouring, drinking yoghurt,
strawberries, frozen yoghurt and
vanilla in a blender and process
until smooth.
2 Pour over lots of ice to serve.

NUTRITION: Protein 10 g; Fat 5.5 g;
Carbohydrate 20 g; Dietary Fibre 2.75 g;
Cholesterol 25 g; 725 kJ (175 cal)

CHOCOHOLIC THICKSHAKE

Preparation time: 5 minutes
Makes 2 x 250 ml glasses

1/2 cup (125 ml) cold milk
50 g dark chocolate, grated
2 tablespoons chocolate syrup
2 tablespoons cream
4 scoops chocolate ice cream
2 scoops chocolate ice cream, extra
grated dark chocolate, extra, to serve

1 Blend the milk, chocolate, syrup,
cream and ice cream in a blender
until smooth.
2 Pour into chilled glasses. Top each
glass with a scoop of ice cream and
sprinkle with grated chocolate.

NUTRITION: Protein 6 g; Fat 25 g;
Carbohydrate 40 g; Dietary Fibre 0 g;
Cholesterol 49 g; 1591 kJ (380 cal)

Index

American iced tea, 49
apple & blackberry
cordial, 14
apple & cinnamon herbal
tea infusion, 18
apricot tofu smoothie, 60
apricot whip, 12

banana, big bold, 21
banana date smoothie, 13
banana passion, 28
banana soy latte, 10
berry & cherry punch, 55
big bold banana, 21
bitter lemon cordial, 14
blackcurrant & apple
shake, 52
bla   12
blue
blueberry starter, 38
breakfast shake, 49

caramel shake, 44
carrot cocktail, 4
celery, tomato & parsley
juice, 35
choc caramel smoothie, 57
choc cherry smoothie, 56
chocoholic thickshake, 63
chocolate mint thickshake,
decadent swirled, 60
chocolate shake, double, 44
cinnamon & custard shake,
56
coconut & lime lassi, 62
coconut & passionfruit
smoothie, 57
cordials, 14–15
cranberry & vanilla ice
cream spider, 6

decadent swirled chocolate
mint thickshake, 60
dinner in a glass, 39
double chocolate shake, 44

Earl Grey summer tea, 58

fennel & orange juice, 34
fresh pineapple juice with
mandarin sorbet, 4

fruit juice, morning
blended, 48
fruit spritzer, 24

ginger, lemon & mint
soother, 4
grapefruit and lemon
sorbet fizz, ruby, 18
green apple & lemon
thirst quencher, 51
green punch, 35

Hawaiian crush, 32
homemade lemonade, 28
honeycomb smoothie, 52
honeydew melon &
passionfruit, 50

ice cubes, 26–27
iced chocolate, 29
iced honeyed coffee, 24
iced lemon & peppermint
tea, 32
iced mint tea, 40
iced tea, American, 49
island blend, 62
island shake, 24

lavender & rose
lemonade, 52
lemon barley water, 23
lemon grass tea, 30
lemon, lime & soda with
citrus ice cubes, 3
lemonade, homemade, 28

malted vanilla shake, 45
mandarin & mango chill, 20
mango smoothie with
fresh berries, 13
melon freezie, 2
melon shake, 7
milk shakes, 44–45
mint julep, 59
mixed berry & lemonade
fizz, 43
morning blended fruit,
juice, 48

orange & cardamom
herbal tea, 16
orange & ginger tea cooler,
22
orange ice cream soda, 46

papaya & orange
smoothie, 37
passionfruit & coconut
cordial, 15
passionfruit ice cream
soda, 48
passionfruit lime crush, 10
passionfruit & vanilla ice
cream whip, 6
peachy egg nog, 8
peachy keen, 10
peanut choc power, 42
pear & mint frappé, 60
pear, apple & ginger juice,
42
pineapple & coconut iced
drink, 36
pineapple & pawpaw juice,
54
pineapple delight, 55
pineapple juice with
mandarin sorbet, fresh, 4
pineapple kick, 43
plum & prune tang, 21
punches, 54–55

raspberry & apple juice, 32
raspberry cordial, 15
raspberry lemonade, 31
ruby grapefruit & lemon
sorbet fizz, 18

smoothberry, 29
sparkling punch, 54
sports shake, 38
spring clean your body, 41
strawberry shake, 45
summer buttermilk
smoothie, 9
summer de-tox, 46
summer strawberry
smoothie, 63

too good for you, 34

virgin mary, 17

watermelon breakfast
juice, 39
watermelon smoothie, 7
wild berries, 20

yoghurt & honey
smoothie, 46